NFL Teams

BALTIMORE RAVENS

KENNY ABDO

Fly!
An Imprint of Abdo Zoom
abdobooks.com

abdobooks.com

Published by Abdo Zoom, a division of ABDO, P.O. Box 398166, Minneapolis, Minnesota 55439. Copyright © 2022 by Abdo Consulting Group, Inc. International copyrights reserved in all countries. No part of this book may be reproduced in any form without written permission from the publisher. Fly!™ is a trademark and logo of Abdo Zoom.

Printed in the United States of America, North Mankato, Minnesota.
052021
092021

THIS BOOK CONTAINS RECYCLED MATERIALS

Photo Credits: AP Images, iStock, Shutterstock PREMIER
Production Contributors: Kenny Abdo, Jennie Forsberg, Grace Hansen
Design Contributors: Candice Keimig, Neil Klinepier

Library of Congress Control Number: 2020919475

Publisher's Cataloging-in-Publication Data

Names: Abdo, Kenny, author.
Title: Baltimore Ravens / by Kenny Abdo
Description: Minneapolis, Minnesota : Abdo Zoom, 2022 | Series: NFL teams | Includes online resources and index.
Identifiers: ISBN 9781098224530 (lib. bdg.) | ISBN 9781098225476 (ebook) | ISBN 9781098225940 (Read-to-Me ebook)
Subjects: LCSH: Baltimore Ravens (Football team)--Juvenile literature. | National Football League--Juvenile literature. | Football teams--Juvenile literature. | American football--Juvenile literature. | Professional sports--Juvenile literature.
Classification: DDC 796.33264--dc23

TABLE OF CONTENTS

Baltimore Ravens 4

Kick Off 8

Team Recaps 14

Hall of Fame 24

Glossary 30

Online Resources 31

Index 32

BALTIMORE RAVENS

Named after Edgar Allen Poe's famous poem, the Baltimore Ravens are a tough and intimidating team.

5

6

Earning two Vince Lombardi trophies and two **Super Bowl** rings, the Ravens have more than proven themselves as champions of the game.

KICK OFF

Cleveland Browns owner Art Modell moved his team from Ohio to Baltimore, Maryland, in 1995. Fans voted "Ravens" to be the new team name.

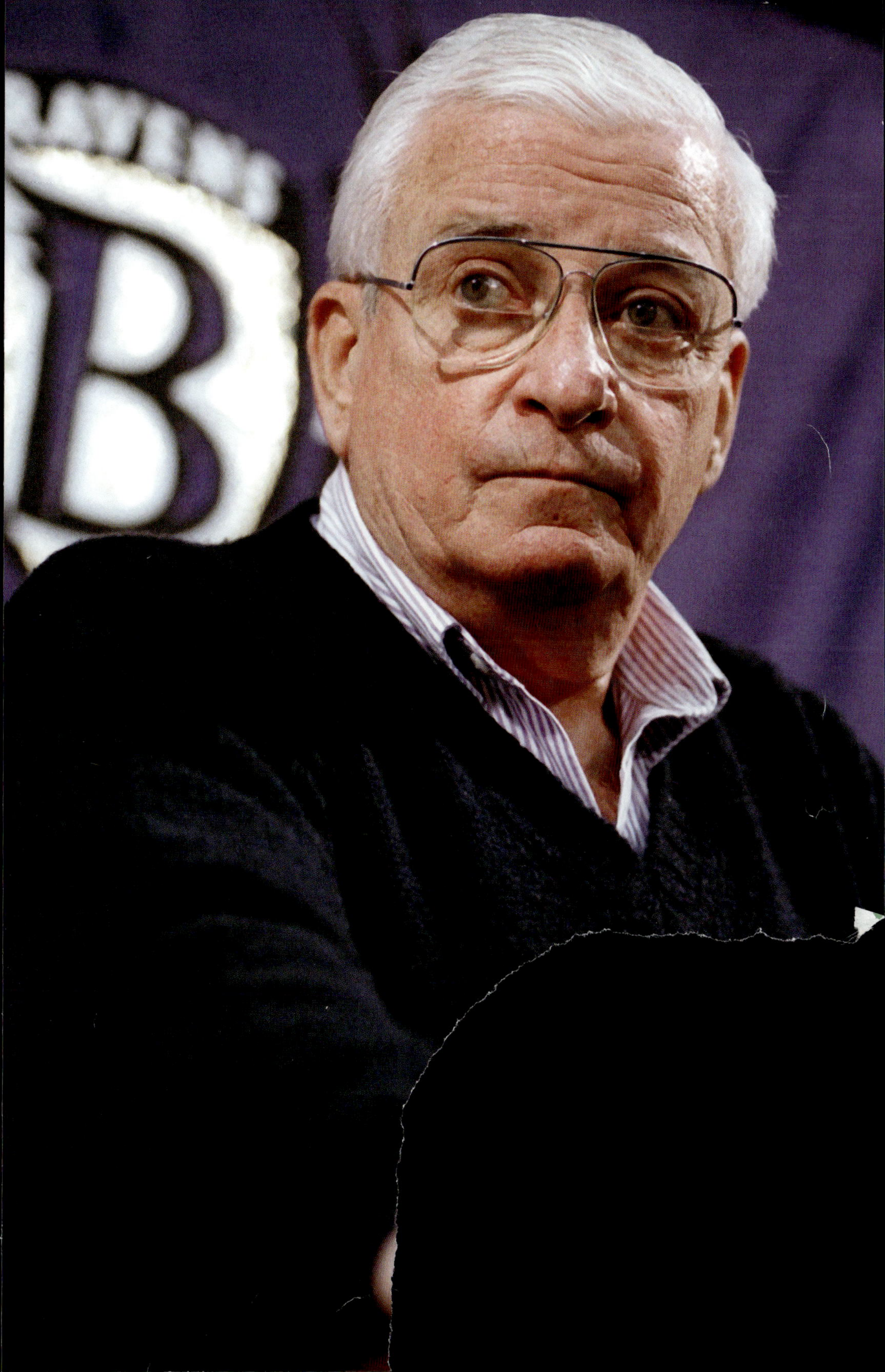

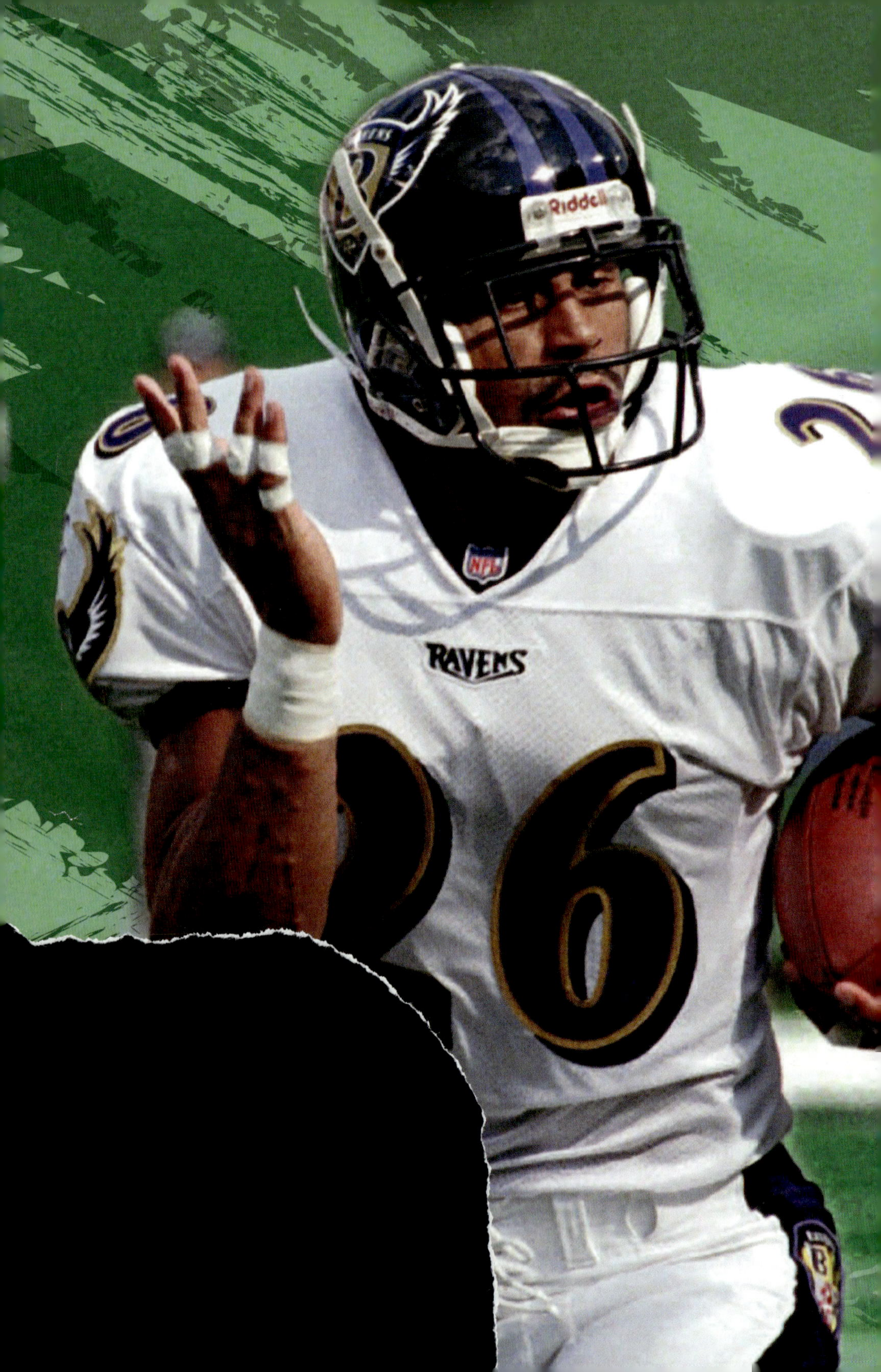
Riddell
NFL
RAVENS
26

The Ravens played their first game in 1996. The team had a losing record its first three seasons.

Brian Billick became head coach in 1999. In the 2000 season, the Ravens won 12 regular-season games, two playoffs, and the **AFC championship**.

13

TEAM RECAPS

The Ravens went to **Super Bowl** XXXV. They beat the New York Giants 34 to 7! Linebacker Ray Lewis was named Super Bowl **MVP**. Lewis also earned Defensive Player of the Year for the 2000 season.

16

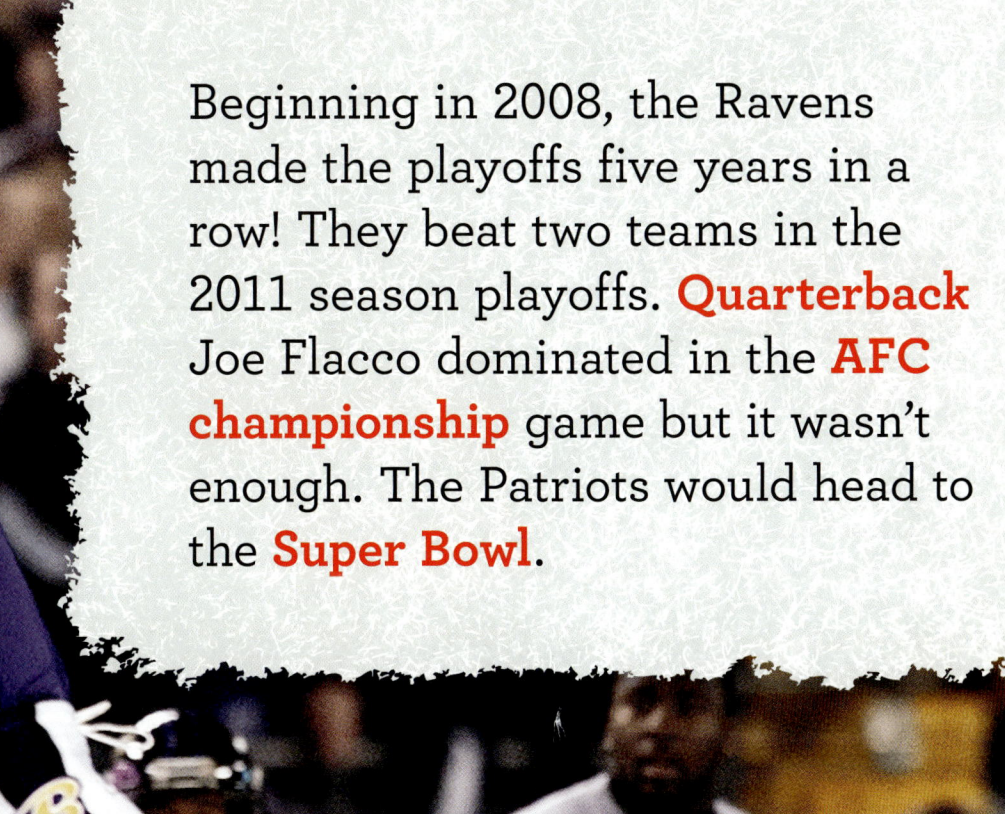

Beginning in 2008, the Ravens made the playoffs five years in a row! They beat two teams in the 2011 season playoffs. **Quarterback** Joe Flacco dominated in the **AFC championship** game but it wasn't enough. The Patriots would head to the **Super Bowl**.

18

The Ravens would redeem themselves in the 2012 season with a trip to the **Super Bowl**. They beat the San Francisco 49ers 34 to 31! Flacco was named Super Bowl **MVP**.

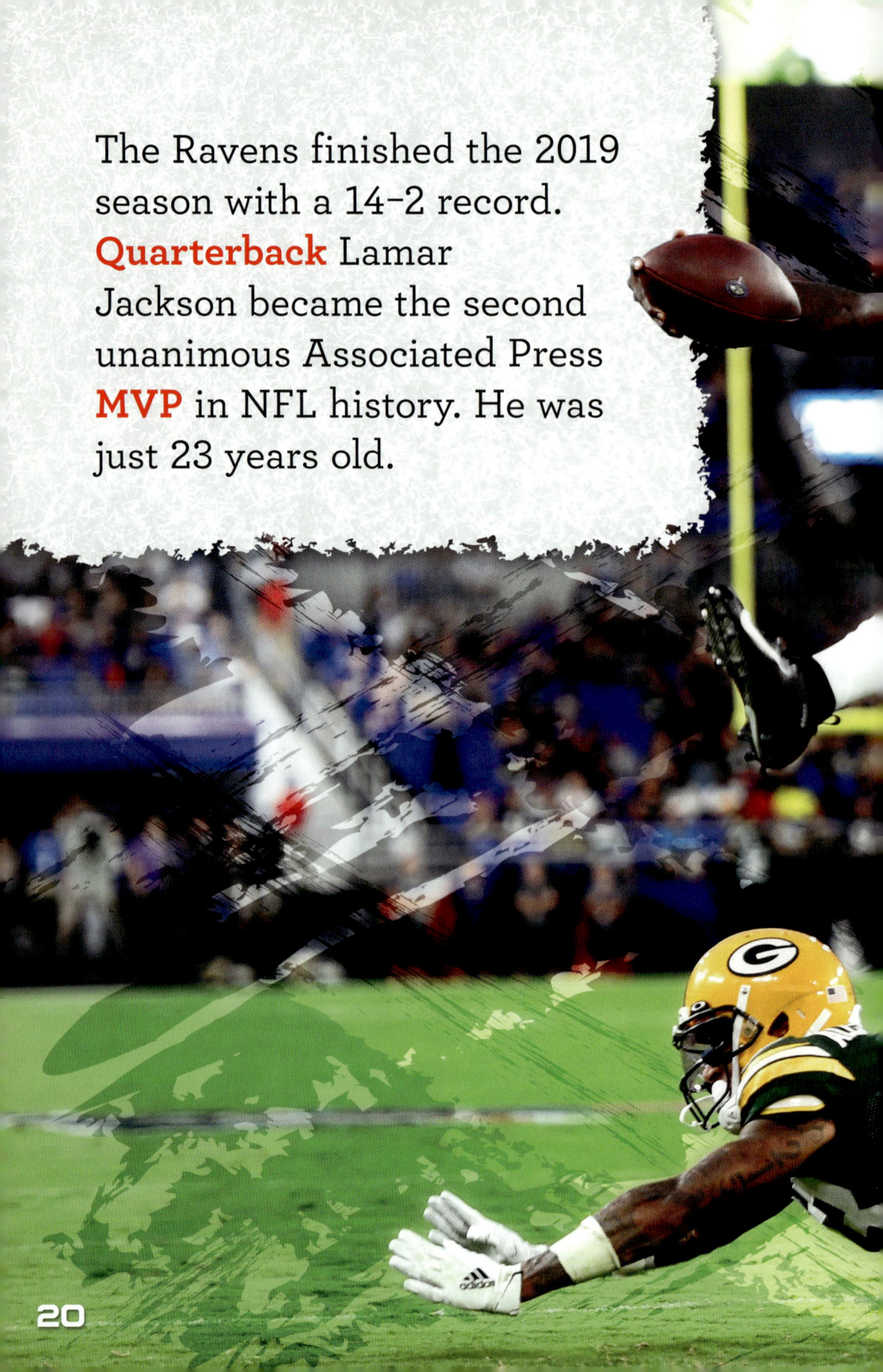

The Ravens finished the 2019 season with a 14-2 record. **Quarterback** Lamar Jackson became the second unanimous Associated Press **MVP** in NFL history. He was just 23 years old.

21

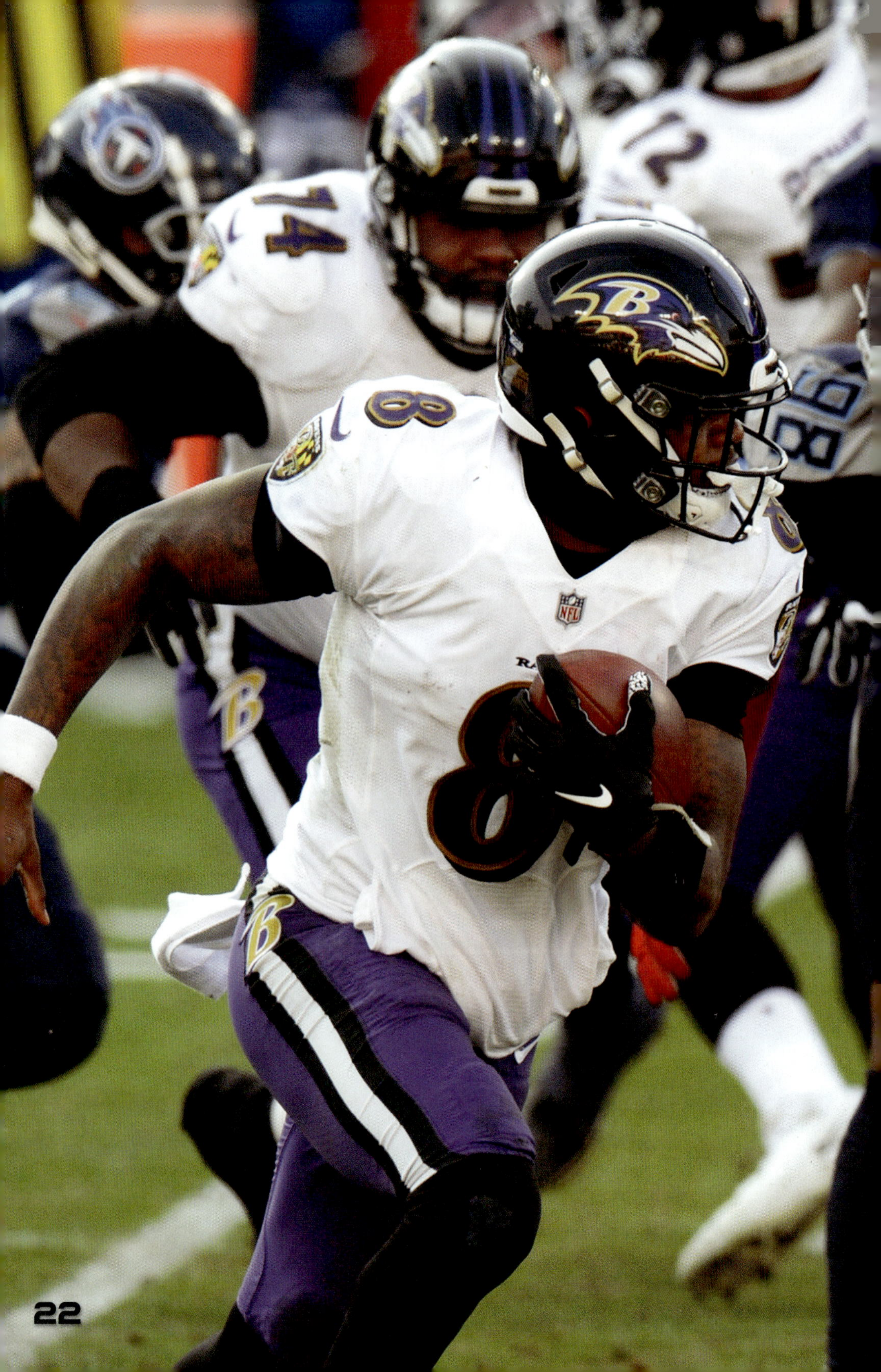

The Ravens beat the Titans in a 2020 Wild Card playoff game 20-13. It was Lamar Jackson's first career playoff victory! It was also the Raven's first playoff win since the 2014 season.

HALL OF FAME

Matt Stover joined the Ravens in 1996. Stover scored every point for the Ravens in five straight games in 2000. He helped the Ravens make it to **Super Bowl** XXXV. Stover is the team's all-time leader in extra points and field goals with 1,464 points.

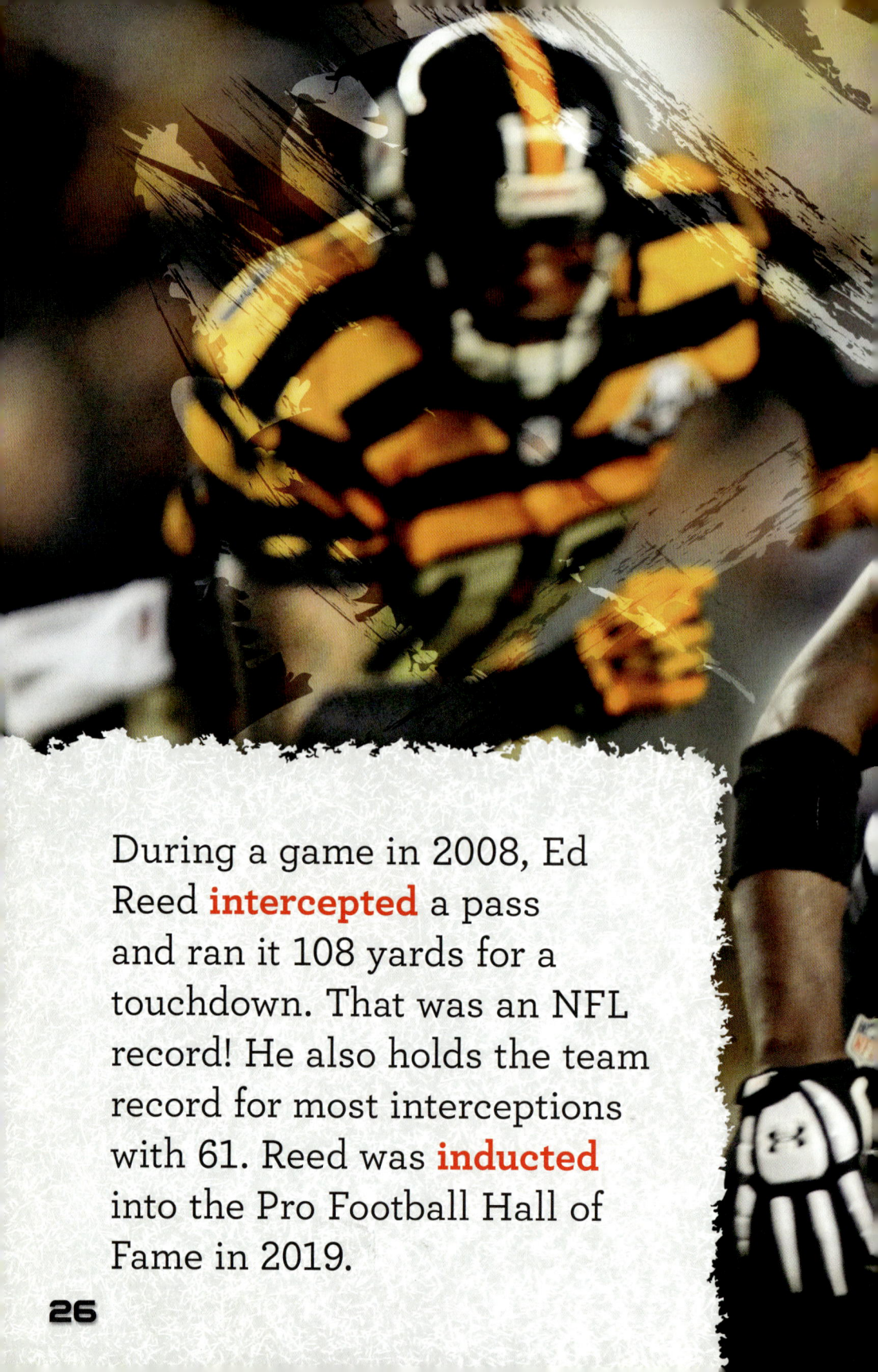

During a game in 2008, Ed Reed **intercepted** a pass and ran it 108 yards for a touchdown. That was an NFL record! He also holds the team record for most interceptions with 61. Reed was **inducted** into the Pro Football Hall of Fame in 2019.

27

28

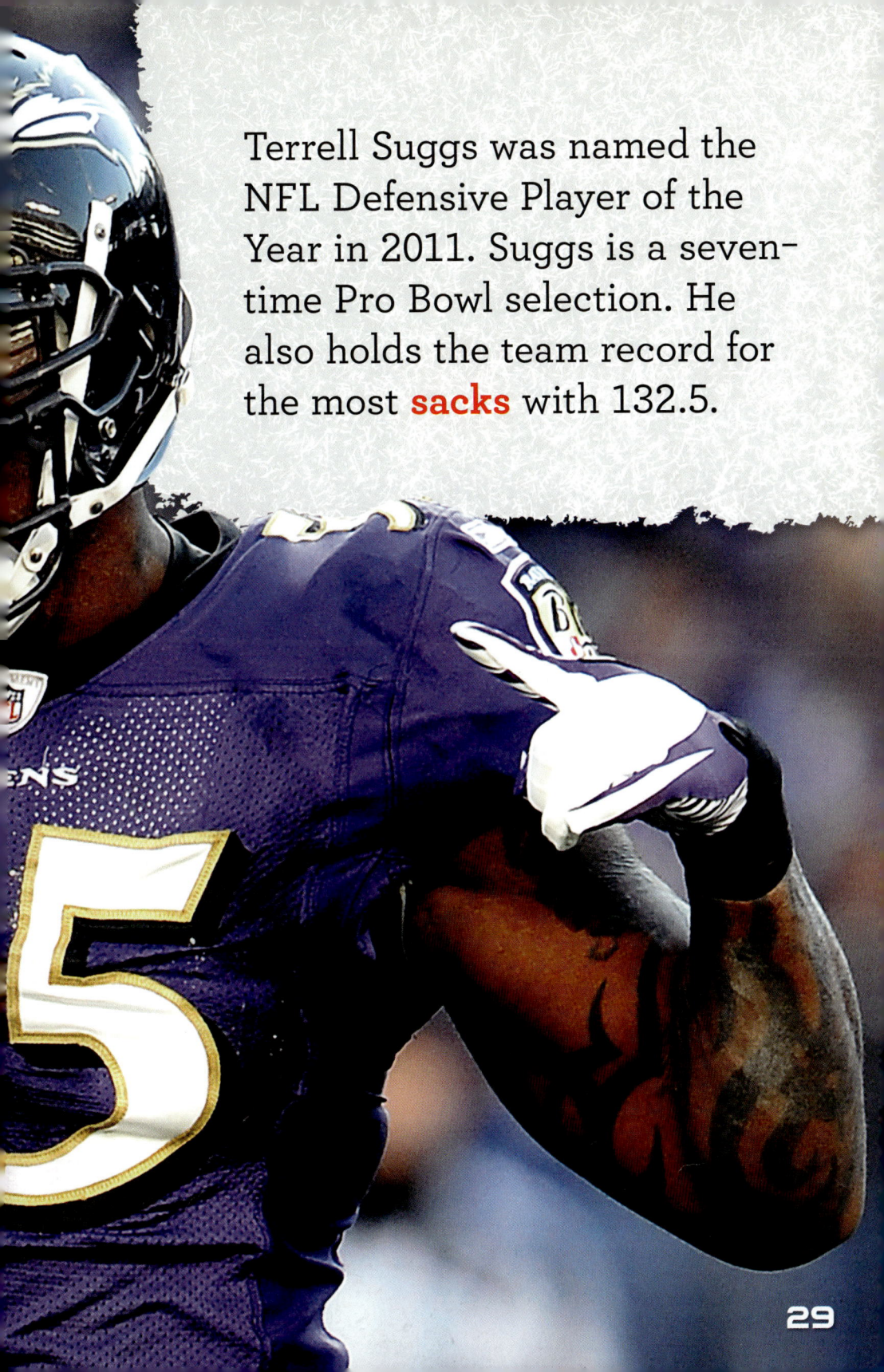

Terrell Suggs was named the NFL Defensive Player of the Year in 2011. Suggs is a seven-time Pro Bowl selection. He also holds the team record for the most **sacks** with 132.5.

GLOSSARY

American Football Conference (AFC) – one of two major conferences of the NFL. Each conference contains 16 teams split into four divisions. The winner of the AFC championship plays the NFC.

championship – a game held to find a first-place winner.

induct – to admit someone as a member of an organization.

interception – when a player catches a pass that was meant for the other team's player.

MVP – short for "most valuable player," an award given in sports to a player who has performed the best in a game or series.

quarterback – the player on the offensive team that directs teammates in their play.

sack – when a quarterback is tackled behind the line of scrimmage while still in possession of the ball.

Super Bowl – the NFL championship game, played once a year.

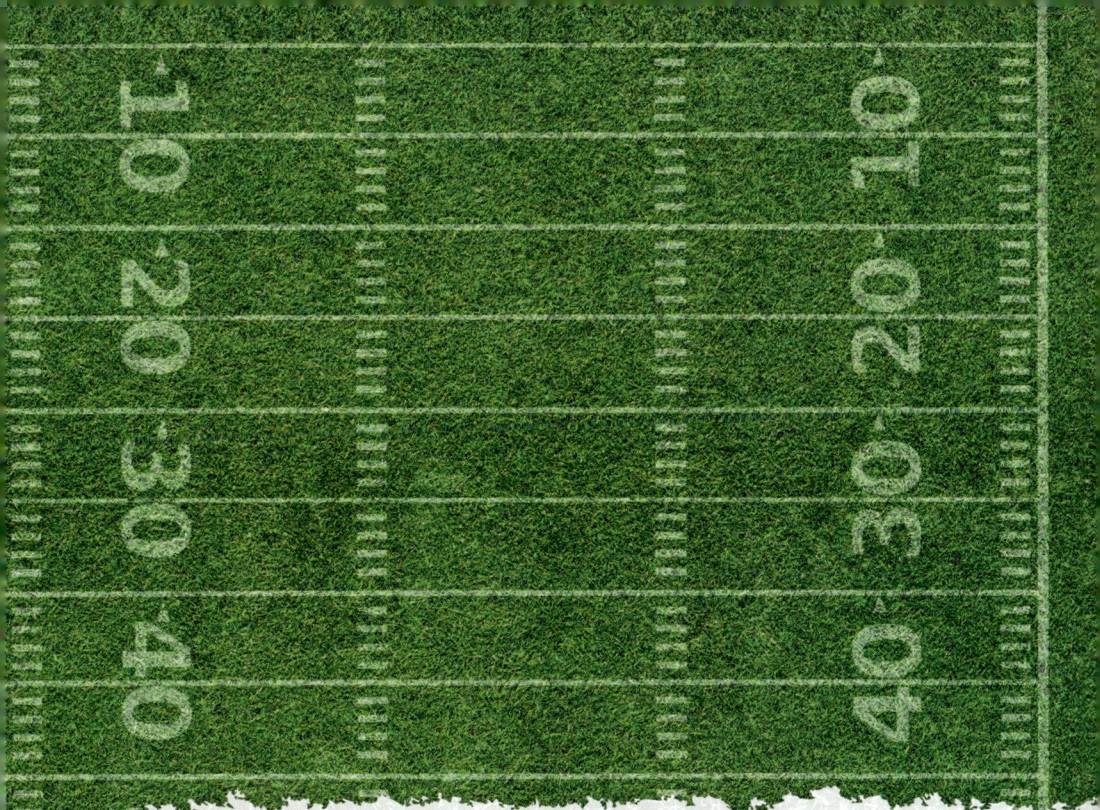

ONLINE RESOURCES

Booklinks
NONFICTION NETWORK
FREE! ONLINE NONFICTION RESOURCES

To learn more about the Baltimore Ravens, please visit **abdobooklinks.com** or scan this QR code. These links are routinely monitored and updated to provide the most current information available.

INDEX

49ers (teams) 19

Billick, Brian 12

Browns (team) 8

championships 12, 15, 17, 19, 23

Flacco, Joe 17, 19

Giants (team) 15

Jackson, Lamar 20, 23

Lewis, Ray 15

Modell, Art 8

Ohio 8

Patriots (team) 17

Poe, Edgar Allen 4

Reed, Ed 26

Stover, Matt 25

Suggs, Terrell 29

Titans (team) 21

Vince Lombardi Trophy 7